Jackpine Sonnets

Also by Milton Acorn

> In Love and Anger (1956)
> Against a League of Liars (1960)
> The Brain's the Target (1960)
> Jawbreakers (1963)
> 58 Poems by Milton Acorn (1963),
>   a Special Edition of "Fiddlehead"
> I've Tasted My Blood (1969)
> More Poems for People (1972)
> The Island Means Minago (1975)
> Numerous Anthology Appearances
> The Road to Charlottetown — a play (1977)
>   with Cedric Smith

Copyright © 1977 Milton Acorn

Jackpine Sonnets   ISBN 0-88791-007-6 bd.
                    ISBN 0-88791-005-X pa.
Milton Acorn

Steel Rail Educational Publishing
P.O. Box 6813, Station A
Toronto, Ontario
M5W 1X6

Typesetting by Zeus Phototype
Printing by Webcom Limited

Jackpine Sonnets

Milton Acorn

Steel Rail Educational Publishing
Toronto, Canada
1977

Steel Rail Educational Publishing

Publishing for the People

Steel Rail Educational Publishing is incorporated as a corporation without share capital and is run by the Steel Rail Collective.

The main thrust of Steel Rail is to search for and publish books written by Canadians, about Canada and the Canadian people's struggles throughout their history, and international titles of interest and value. Steel Rail is a house through which people can exchange ideas and publish materials that might not otherwise be published.

Canadian Catalogue in Publication Data
Acorn, Milton, 1923-
    Jackpine sonnets

ISBN 0-88791-007-6 bd.   ISBN 0-88791-005-X pa.

I. Title.

PS8501.C64J28   C811'.5'4   C77-001326-0
PR9199.3.A18J28

As Shakespeare would say "To the Onlie
Begetter of these Poems"
                    Kenneth Leslie

I sail by stubborn stars. Let rocks take heed:
and if I sink; then sinking be my creed.
                    K.L.

That is not dead which can forever lie
And through strange ages even death may die.
                    H.P. Lovecraft

Acknowledgements

To Joyce Wayne, editor, who worked so closely with the author beginning well before there was a complete manuscript that it would almost amount to collaboration.

To Errol Sharpe, Manager of Steel Rail, without whose remorseless tyranny and attention to details this book might never have been completed.

To members of the Steel Rail Editorial Committee, especially Marion Endicott and Linda Capacchione, who made publication in this form possible.

Cover design from a drawing *"Jackpine — a variation on Lismer"*, by Robert Kell.

Contents

By Still More Stubborn Stars

(for Kenneth Leslie)

There are men who can see one star break
Momentarily through a rake of clouds;
Guess which it is and thereupon stake
Course, life and many more thumping loud
Human pulses on a line more tenuous
Through an incoherent stagger of shocks,
Than one by which a new spider launches
His wee red splot of life over world-tops.
By still more stubborn stars, against still more
Dreadful collisions, meaner misdirections
(loud and willing liars calling the score)
Do I make aim to steer this lusty pen
So finely shaped like spear or phallus
To save or kill as right as it fertilizes.

The Round of Beer

"In the beginning was the lie!" one thumped
"And lie by lie each new yap ate the last!"

"Don't talk politics," his old friend grumped,
"A logger's life is short. Grab it going past!"

"Listen ape," his chum said — but was interrupted
By their new acquaintance, who braved:
"You're looking at time all arse-backward
— future to present — no offense . . .
Yesterday's truth becomes today's non-sense."

"Here we have a radical philosopher"
Said number two: "Hark!
I hear a bugle!" Shifting rump
He made the glassware ring with a hoarded fart

Then I saw the party of the third part
Set his grin up for a target
"To refute all pessimism," he said, "I live . . .
As proof of life — Well what about yours?
You bet your life I prize the life I bet."

The Montreal Fan

When Les Habitants glide onto the ice
A great bird out of time unruffles wings.
Every throat there, is possessed by a spirit
So greetings rise from an angelic chorus.
Less a team itself than a living spirit
I'm told and want to believe
That, on a sheet of clear ice, each man
Can skate his name, cleanly as by hand.
Dashes represent the years when they don't own the cup.

I've seen with these two eyes, one second fractioned
By three cracking passes — the fourth shot a goal.
What would you call this but a miracle?
Popular thunder swells impatient.
The lions have arrived! Where are the Christians?

Rose in Absence

The orgasm doesn't end. This moment
Is like mated swallows, spinning strands of time;
Miniature cyclones in my breath
Where exhalations from two nostrils blend.
I hear a tern call, and call back for luck
To you as well . . . shucked off a thousand miles
From Island dirt into Toronto grime.

There was a man who told me dialectics
Contradicted mathematical laws.
I should tell him love's equally wicked.
In a love-gift, what the hell's lost?

No end of curses to the ones who curse
Fate's loveliest joke, cutting to tit-bits
The worse parts of existence, tinting
This blue earthly sky with martian rose.
The clouds are you, the chiming sea your voice;
Each stone your tooth, and all the better for it.

Tirade by Way of Introduction

When there comes one of those times in the affairs of human and lesser fauna — there being poets in both categories — that a great flutterby rush is seen flying all one direction; the greying but still dangerous poet of prey wheels his head to look sardonically at all this traffic — without the slightest urge to join. He takes off with power and practiced strokes in the direction from which the mob fled. Something's frightening the little dears; and that which frightens them is his provender. This scramble into scrambled verse (which can no longer be called free because freedom requires knowledge of one's trade, and something to work with) is not an advance, not even a retreat. It is a rout.

Like the mad Hamlet the poets in their majority have posed themselves the insane question — to be or not to be? It is preposterous on the face of it, as Old Shakes no doubt intended. Later a poet tried to dodge the question, "Poetry must not mean — but be . . . "

But of course it's impossible to put a grammatically arranged plot of words together without meaning something, however obscure. So this awful inevitability is dodged by not putting words together in any sensible way.

Why? These are interesting times. Some like them, some don't like them. Most people now going into poetry do so to escape the interest of the times.

They've taken the fate of Neruda to heart and cried "Not me! Not innocent little me!" But of course they are not innocent. Aware that anything they put down in print may be held against them, they decide to put nothing down — but still print. Thus they put a brake on the gathering interest in poetry. Innocent audiences come for miles to hear what is advertised as poetry, and go away resolved never to inflict such appalling torture as Judge Boring and his like pander, on themselves again.

In this volume I do acknowledge that poetry is in a state of crisis and offer a partial prescription. About the content of my poetry I'll say nothing here. Everyone knows I'm an ideological poet and my central ideology is Marxism-Leninism. Everyone knows or should know I'm a patriotic poet and my patriotism is not contrary to Marxism-Leninism. The fakers who declare that all patriotism is bad and against Marxism-Leninism, can be refuted chapter and verse from the classics of the science. I'll not bother to repeat one smidgeon of those refutations. There are the books.

* * *

The present crisis in poetry traces back to that time in another country when Shelley said:

> The world's great age begins anew
> The golden years return
> The earth doth like a snake renew
> Her winter weeds outworn . . .
> Heaven smiles and faiths and empires gleam
> Like mists in a dissolving dream.

Shelley was operating under the difficulty of trying to speak in the people's language when he didn't well understand it himself. No one could understand it was in a furious process of change due to the spread of education — from books which spoke in the language of the rulers — among the workers. It was first spread by the workers themselves. Later, for obvious reasons, the state took over. Thus his mode of speech sounds a little flighty.

The meat of it is still there. He predicts the great age of wonders in which we now live. In this and other poems he predicts it will be an age, not only of great human advance, but also great conflict. Note that he calls the earth a "snake." Beautiful and dangerous.

Shelley of course lived in the Modern Age (with letters capitalized — indicating that the age was not simply modern in the sense of being the then-now age, but Modern in the sense that Modern was the name of the age). There was great change in his time and the illusion that all change is progress was getting a stronger and stronger hold on men's minds.

That age is over. This is the Romantic Age, where all things are possible, but we no longer consider all change good.

Shelley, of course, was preceded by other Romantics and pre-Romantics. Far up among the latter is to be counted Robert Burns — particularly with a poem which at first reading sounds common, but gathers deeper significance as it's read again:

14

Now let us pray that come it may
As come it will for a' that
That sense and worth o'er a' the earth
Shall bear the gree for a' that
For a' that and a' that
That man to man the warld o'er
Shall brithers be for a' that
For a' that and a' that
It's comin' yet! For a' that.

Writing a quaint blend of English and Old Scots which was his native dialect, Burns is almost impossible to transcribe from memory. On top of that I've taken the liberty of switching lines about in a manner I'm sure Burns would have agreed with.

The Romantic poets came long before the present Romantic Age. Inevitably the wave declines, and the so-called later romantics were hardly romantics at all. But true romanticism set one good foot in Canada and stomped hard. Only many decades afterwards was it recognized that a form of poetry derived from romanticism had been the main line in Canadian poetry since the 1840's.

This realization was marked by an event in which I was involved. After a particularly mean and false decision of the Canada Council as to who was to get the GG (governor general's award) for 1969, the majority of the good poets rallied — gave me the CANADIAN POETS AWARD, and on the reverse side of the medal was imprinted the legend THE PEOPLE'S POET.

There had been people's poets before, including Dorothy Livesay — still extant. She had once written a book POEMS FOR PEOPLE and I hastened to remind them of the facts of history by calling my following book MORE POEMS FOR PEOPLE. I had her permission and it was dedicated to her.

Incidentally my "People's Poet" award was confirmed by my 'winning' of the GG (Canada still being a democracy, albeit bourgeois, some attention has to be paid to the real state of things) early this year. The book for which I won that trivial bauble was a spirited attack on the complete mis-writing of Canadian history, using Minago (P.E.I.) as an example.

Win the GG? Why I tore it from their hands, breaking every finger one by one! I was criticised by self-proclaimed proletarians for accepting the GG. The fact was that 5,000 dollars went with it. What proletarian ever snatched back his hand when the boss handed him his paycheck, however mean? I've earned everything

I've got, and what is unjustly not given me, I take.

Where the boss is ashamed to show his face, he orders out the auxiliaries. A purportedly radical magazine, ALIVE (?) which specializes in savage attacks on radicals, called me a degenerate. But another poet, when he read that column of filth, said he was consumed with envy . . . for the 'degenerate' label is a crown of honour for a poet . . . it means you're starting to draw blood — not just in the poetic community.

*   *   *

What were other poets doing all this time? Some were doing good things. Most were putting on abominable performances.

I began to tackle the pressing problems of Canadian poetry; beginning my Jackpine Sonnets. Previously my books have been noted for a variety of stylistic types. I doubt if through all those years I wrote more than three poems altogether in the same mode. Practically all were examples of formal elegance, used in a free fashion.

Now I thank David Donnel, a fine poet who kept my secret for many years after he'd detected it. Many or most of those stylistic forms (not the content) were 'swipes'. It was a time of poetic invention all over the world. Many good translations reached us. I studied them well and brought out my own variations of the forms. When I did actually plagiarize a poem, I did it honestly — that is, put the name of the original author in brackets and italics, under the poem. You'll see an example of such an honest plagiarization in this book . . . thus — (*after Hikmet*). Hikmet was a Turkish Communist poet whose ideas were brilliant, but whose performance didn't often come up to the conception. He is one of the most copied poets on Earth — and not always honestly. Of course, in such a rewriting you make some essential change. If it's a straight repeat in another language it goes down as a translation.

All the time I tried to write sonnets. They fascinated me. Some were actually successful and published, but were not among my happier performances.

Was something wrong with me? I mused. Impossible! There must be something wrong with the sonnet.

In a college dictionary which comes to hand, a sonnet is designated as *a poem with fourteen lines*. That definition is pitiful.

A sonnet is a short poem with a dialectical play of argument. It was not always limited to fourteen lines. That just came to be accepted because, I'm certain, longer types, and likely shorter types too, became victims of the rigidity of the sonnet form.

There's what we call The Shakespearian Sonnet. Then there's the Miltonic Sonnet, not broken up into verses, but giving the author a freer choice of the rhyme-scheme. This I believe was actually invented by that other Milton.

MILTON'S ON HIS BLINDNESS SONNET HAS THIRTEEN LINES! Don't rush to get a book to check up. You'll count fourteen lines there, but closer examination reveals one half-line and then another half which are pure sluff — put in to bring up the line-count.

But as I traced the sonnet up through history I began detecting the stretches and strains as the sonnet tried to break out of its iron chains. The problem of that *weak-stress* first syllable, for instance. It plays hell with run-on lines . . . and oh yes I saw poets just dropping it to leave a line of nine syllables.

Who would ever notice?

But then there was also the problem of translation. Hard enough to write a regular sonnet (*almost* regular — none are quite) but to translate one and keep the rhyme-scheme! Translators led the way to the Jackpine Sonnet: saying oh to hell with it, keeping the original meaning as much as possible, while making the rhyme-scheme irregular. Finally Robert Lowell gave himself the chance of a lifetime. Grabbing the skunk by the tail, he wrote irregular sonnets and didn't care who blamed him. A man heroic enough to boycott a White House reception to protest the Vietnam War has nerve enough for anything.

Bravo for that! Robert Lowell. But why did you make your irregular sonnets so obscure?

Besides that, the poor fool forgot to plant a sign beside his invention — didn't give it a name. Of course I haven't got the nerve to give the Lowellian Sonnet my own name. There already is a Miltonic Sonnet. As for the Acornic Sonnet . . . It sounds awful. So I have named it after one of my favourite trees — the Jackpine, which can grow in any earth in which you plant it, so long as it's not crowded: can be a puny but tough battle-scarred veteran clinging to an impossible cliffside, or a proud giant in a pasture. Unlike other conifers *it grows at opportunity*, having no set form. Thus with its solid-looking needle-foliage, it makes all sorts of evocative shapes. No wonder the eastern Indians had no totem poles. We had Jackpines . . . .

> *If it looks like nothing on Earth — not even a Jackpine*
> *It must be a Jackpine . . . Or a Canadian.*

Jackpines are so individual they can be used as landmarks, no matter how many other trees are around. Therefore I call my free form sonnet The Jackpine, and the book JACKPINE SONNETS . . . to make a landmark in the history of poetry.

Poetasters, fearful worms who disgrace poetry with poems, so-called, having neither shape or substance . . .
You call me arrogant!
You who stand
before audiences boring them into catatonia with your unspeaking products. Who callously read over your time, crowding other poets off the list. You call me arrogant! Bullshit! I call you horses arses!

Do I speak plainly enough? I dread not. In the words of our memorable — if nothing else, Prime Minister: *Mange la merde* — don't void it from your mouths and expect your audiences to eat it.
Conserve
paper. Don't print your poems unless you've got something to say. Say anything. Otherwise save the material for something useful, like wiping rectums, blowing noses, padding baby's buttocks.

At the start of my Jackpine Sonnet campaign first I stuck to the fourteen-line formula but considered that if the sonnet would not stop at fourteen lines I shouldn't truncate it. I wrote things up to twenty lines which still looked and sounded like sonnets. I re-arranged the rhyme-schemes — well hardly arranged. I just thought if the first line ended with a word like, for instance, 'shit', and no rhyme occurred immediately, don't panic; but let four lines pass before worrying about the virtues of 'habit', and such.

Make up for this by using internal, as well as external, rhymes to keep the flow. Also if there's no rhyme use an assonance. Try using it to keep the rhyme alive in order to come up with a true rhyme further on. There's also a trick of interweaving external and internal rhymes and assonances.

Also I tried, in the division of the sonnet verses — when I cut in verses — to put the six-line verse first and the eight-line second. This too had been done before, in fact I believe it's quite orthodox. I also devised other ways to cut up sonnets into verses, 4-6-4, for example, which I may have originated. Also irregular verses, which were not new either. The Jackpine had been growing for a long time. I had   resolved from the first to make a line any length I liked. But I found the ideal line to be, roughly, between 7 and 13 syllables.

But the problem of the set number of lines for a sonnet remained. It could not be banished by the vague non-injunction that if a sonnet refused to stop at fourteen lines — why force it? Or if a sonnet refused to stretch to fourteen lines — why force it? The fourteen-line compulsion has a lot of historical weight behind it. Well then, let's take a look at the thirteen-line problem.

I called up thoughts of history concerning the number thirteen. I drew much on my feeble knowledge of mathematics. Why does the number 13 obsess us so? In some cultures it is considered unlucky, in others lucky. Thirteen is known as a baker's dozen — because bakers used to put thirteen bits of whatever in a package to avoid cheating even by accident, because in those days there were fearful penalties for giving a short count.

Thirteen was the number of Jesus and the twelve apostles. One turned out to be a traitor. The one selected in his place became the first Christian martyr (that's an aside on the question of unluckiness . . . actually, by the way, there were thirteen apostles when you count Mary Magdalene). Thirteen was the number of the witch's coven — perhaps because thirteen was the highest prime number of persons in which you could be reasonably sure of everyone.

That's it! Thirteen is a prime number.

And fourteen is the sum of two sevens, a prime sum of a prime.

A squad in the Russian army comprises twelve men and a sergeant. If you lose half you still have a squad. Also, if there were more, some of the men would likely not know all their comrades' names . . . embarrassing in any case, but in battle it can be downright disastrous. Unaware at the time that space warfare between American and Russian robot craft had already begun, I even figured out the formation of a spatial fighter squadron. It would be echeloned in three dimensions, not two as with geese and aircraft. The leader would be followed by three branching lines of four craft each. This would also have the advantage of not revealing the internal organization of the squadron to an observer. The next number possessing the same advantage would be seventeen and that would be unwieldy. And what about the celebrated number — twelve — of the British fighter squadron in the Anti-Fascist War? Was that not a euphemism for thirteen? Was 'tail-end charlie' not number thirteen?

If tail-end

charlie went down in flames you knew you were under attack.

I leave that last question open. I don't know . . .

Mad fantasies like these are mental exercises a poet goes through to impress some idea on his mind. Many forget the original intent and concentrate on the fantasies.

Then I was writing thirteen-line sonnets — and the Jackpine broke loose. Prime numbers of lines — that was to be the rule! Fourteen lines permissible still, tradition is not to be forgotten. What about 11 lines! *Alors* . . . In cases when the theme, though still argumentative, wouldn't carry thirteen lines, I did drop to eleven. Think of all the useless verbiage I've sluffed off without even going to the trouble of an abortion. The prime pill did it.

The next prime down from 11 is 7. Impossible for a sonnet, though I do hear rumours that 9 is in some category even rarer than a prime. It's a complementary number, I'm told. What's that? I don't know. Harry the desk-clerk told me about complementary numbers.

Seventeen he said is also complementary. If that's true it has a doubled power — for 17 is the next prime up from 13. To be serious, the necessity for a longer short sonnet has always been felt. Many a sonnet has never seen the day because the 17-line form, and the 19-line form, have not until now been decreed. The 17-line form (see NO MUSIC FROM THE BAR) can be just as concise as a 13 or 14-liner. Also there and in the following 19-line slot a new quality is showing itself. Wasn't the Jackpine form invented to allow new qualities? The next prime, 23, makes for quite a long jump and the temptation to fill out, rather than trim, becomes strong. All I can say is that if your sonnet cuts itself off — click! — at, say line 12, 18 or 20, leave it at that. It's still a Jackpine because you tried. Too many poets don't recognize that *click*.

Are such long things really sonnets? Indeed they are. The term 'sonnet' has been applied to much longer poems.

Finally you come to the point where the prime-number rule can no longer apply. Primes become rarer and rarer as you go up the number series. But then you are writing another kind of poem, a ballad or short epic. The Jackpine principle of irregular rhyme has wider applications than just to sonnets.

"Straight lines are foreign to nature," an instructor in the detection of camouflage told me long ago. That is why my Jackpine rules are regular ones which compel irregularity. It is impossible to divide a prime number into neat, identical packages!

The history of poetry, as that of any art, is often presented as a history of destructions, each generation turning its claws against the last. For obvious reasons, we Canadians can't afford to take that attitude all too seriously.

So speaking of the development of the jackpine sonnet in Canada, the whole history of the sonnet should be touched upon — briefly. The recent attacks on the sonnet are nothing new. It has always been suspect. It is much too much a tool adaptable to political statement . . . which should be the province of statesment and presidents (joke) to ever enjoy the favour of . . . et cetera and so on.

Let me just state that Lampman's Upper (Ottawa) Valley speech has to be taken into account for full comprehension of Archibald Lampman's poetry. Charles G.D. Roberts has both less and more trouble with the voice than Lampman. In a sonnet like THE FROGS, the voice is written in and sings out. In others it is difficult to find any voice. The print lies flat on the page and won't rise.

When we come to the loveliest of our orthodox sonneteers, Kenneth Leslie, the battle for the Canadian voice is being fought, and he is winning it. With the heretical line *"Milk, oatmeal and molasses made my soul"* a mystic is defining the limits of mysticism. In *"A warm rain whispers but the earth knows best"* (two pathetic fallacies on one line — and the sonnet goes on like that) he demonstrates that no poetic rules are absolute. He must have had a hilarious time! In Leslie the jackpine principle is already there; but he uses it inconspicuously and rarely, always wanting to give his readers the impression that what they see is an orthodox sonnet, however unorthodox the content.

He could do this because what was (I hope) to become known as the Jackpine sonnet was already here. Perhaps it was born in Canada. Who knows? Here are some lines from A.M. Klein's SONNET WITH MUSIC — on the defeat of the Spanish Republic.

Upon the piazza, haemophillic dons
delicately lift their sherry in the sun.

Having recovered confiscated land,
and his expropriated smile redeemed,
the magnate too, has doffed his socialized face.
He beams a jocund aftermath to bombs.

Also the priest — alas for such bloodshed ! —
cups plumpish hand to catch uncataschized belch . . .

I've gone far enough with this 'fourteen-line poem with an argument' to catch the beautiful thought-rhyme of 'bombs' and 'belch'. There are other tricks of sonnetry running all through, which definitely define this as a jackpine sonnet.

Cubs sucked milk long before anybody knew of mammals, let alone named them.

Klein's fate was to be worse than Leslie's. The awful backlash of the Imperialists after World War II — the Cold War — was marked by one small incident, among many, the sinking of A.M. Klein into a pathological depression which lasted til his death — twenty years later.

Faced with the same awful pressure which did Klein in, the sonnet went underground. It jackpined! Now the trick was to cut your lines up in an unorthodox way which didn't even seem unorthodox. Reaney and Purdy would keep to a sonnet form til the last line — which would be rudely cut in half. Mandel would write a poem, obviously a sonnet when you come to think of it, with a 4-5-6 verse-pattern . . . fifteen lines, but what the hell?

MacEwen would set an even bolder face on it, by cutting up her verses 4-5-5 . . .

Self, I want you now to be
Violent and without history,
for we've rehearsed too long our ceremonial ballet
and I fear my calm against your exquisite rage.

One doesn't have to agree with the sentiment (which after all is a datum) to appreciate, for one thing, the magnificent thought-rhyme in the word 'rage' against the word 'age' (meaning 'the age') which word is there, though not said.

Remember too that there is really no limit to line-length in the jackpine sonnet . . . halfway down a football field plus the whole length back! By contemporary techniques, lines longer than a page-width have to be printed as two lines — with indications that they are to be read as one. Remember that if you want to go jackpine-hunting yourself.

When discussing the jackpine sonnet with the prime number of lines . . . one is getting onto dangerous ground. Poets are bound to take issue with me if I declare certain of their poems sonnets.

So I'd better just speak for myself. LETTER TO MY RED-HEADED SON was first printed in AGAINST A LEAGUE OF LIARS in 1958. It's often quoted back at me; though never anthologized . . .

> *Young maple leaves, copper with a delicate flush*
> *are taut and hardly bent by the limb-twist breeze*
> *and I'm penetrated by the delight that bore you*
> *and makes fool poets call the spring green.*
>
> *A poet against a league of liars, I know*
> *you'll learn love and honesty from her*
> *who wouldn't learn scorn and left me.*
> *You'll learn, boy, to be as bitter as me*
> *against the men with counterfeit eyes,*
> *their graft and their words: "nigger";*
> *"people not like us" . . . and "bastard."*
>
> *Fool poets call the spring green, but I*
> *a poet, know I can't give you to yourself*
> *— only what I know of myself: that*
> *nothing I've done, no poem, stand,*
> *thought or act of love, hasn't called for*
> *another, stronger deed, or I've lost it.*

If that's not a jackpine sonnet, of seventeen lines, I don't know what it is. Though the poem stands, without apology, as a datum of the age. I think I'll follow my custom of including an old poem — for luck — in each book by including a revision (another take — rather) of this sonnet in JACKPINE SONNETS.

In an old fort back of the earlier of the two Roman walls, in Britain, one-half of a pair of dice has been dug up. It was loaded. Most fossilized dice do turn out to be loaded, but that's because loaded dice were those most apt to be fossilized — along with their owners.

Poets who expect their poetry to live, both in the present and future, must learn again how to load their poems. There are always new ways . . .

* * *

One caution . . . . I am *not* officially announcing the death of the old regular sonnet. I know its death has been declared in every generation for that last hundred years. It has not died because it won't. It still won't. In the entire history of poetry no well-established form has ever died. Regular sonnets will be still written when the pyramids are dust. No artifact of humanity has more resilience than poetry.

But I can hear all those chicken-scratchers, audience insulters, etc., screaming with horror. "Why any rules at all? We are anarchists and free, free, free!" Yes you are free to oppress as long as audiences can be lured into halls you so ungainfully grace, held there with the false claim that your awful garbage is good for them.

Aw come on now! Isn't it true you're not anarchists? That designation is just another of your frauds. Your flag is not the black one of valiance to the end, but the white flag of surrender. I have shit black turds and white, and know the difference.

* * *

In this book, JACKPINE SONNETS, will appear a strange word — *realisant*. Don't look for it in the dictionary because it's not there. It's a word coined in one of those discussions with Purdy. It means *romantic* in the real old sense . . . that of the original Romantic poets . . . not of those in the trough of the wave who fatally changed the meaning of the word 'romantic' as applied to poetry. Think of it as meaning 'realistic' but not fanatic about it — 'flexible'. It is a combination of the Anglo-French word 'real' and a diminutive from some other language whose identity my friends dispute.

The Jackpine is realisant. It has a basic form, yes, but grows to any shape that suits the light, suits the winds, suits itself.

Again to those apostates' lyingly naming their stuff 'free verse'. Your cowardice will get you, not as you hope, nowhere; but somewhere bad. In battle it is the brave man pressing forward who is most likely to survive. It's those who fiddle around pre-occupied with fear who most often fall. They're thinking only of themselves — not paying attention. So, when the Yankee torturemen come, your mute betrayal of poetry won't save you. Meanwhile it's just possible I shall be in ambush at some secret spot dealing fearful blows.

Thus the Jackpine Sonnet came out of its cover.

Milton Acorn
May Day 1977

24

Hope Begins Where False Hope Ends

Hope begins where false hope ends:
The strongest hope, made certain to win —
Tool redesigned, perfect in heft and fit.
If you sing in one key with the spheres
Ignoble in no aspect, the mending begins
Of all your losses, breakage, all those errors.

The strongest bone is one broken and mended.
The strongest brain has conceived a fool theory,
Researched, contrived, argued its defense
Then given up in face of evidence;
Or else stayed strong against a rally of prejudice
Because its truth keeps some part unwearied;
Until one hears the music of regiments
Loud in chorus, doctored with that medicine . . .

First Wife Sonnet

Could I forget an arm, a leg, an eye
Which I had once and then had amputated?
If I could do that thing . . . then sure I'd
Deny how dialectically mated
We were . . . one of us the bird and one the air
But which one which? Two tunes in one song
. . . but who the melody, and who in there
To swing wrong when one was right, right when one was wrong?

Maybe that's an incorrect putting of it
And I say this only for argument:
My loved crossed and lost one . . . we fit
So well in our joint seizures, wild entanglements
Our juices must have splattered over planets
Fertilizing alien forget-me-nots.

The Canadian Bank Loan to Chile

Where's the collateral for yehr Chilean loan?
Do ye' think that damned fascist state
Will stand so long against enraged peoples
To guarantee one nickel to yehr dollar?
Hae ye' gone so daft ye' think the Devil's thumbprint
On his oath to maintain eternal evil
Is worth a hollar from a flaming collar?
You, sirs, remind me of Napoleon's words
When such a savage fool as one of yehrselves
Stood before him expecting rewards:
"You stand there proud of an awful crime done;
Splotching the blotter of the French State
With blood you've made to spout for no sane reason:
Worst of all
      Sir Donkey
          you
             have
                made
                   a mistake."

Sonnet Translated From the Gaelic

*(In loving memory of old settlers of Minigo
[Prince Edward Island] whose history has been
most damnably suppressed . . . promising that
the world shall know again of them and their
bold lives.)*

Once blood spattered . . . One lay on the ground
That puddle needed to become a lake.
Let no words follow that one broken sound
Or allow a muted keening to break
Those lips of yours like two red quarter-moons.
Be silent as the dead, for they're all dead.
We meant only to warn . . . Half-swilled-over goons
Couldn't be told. One hard stroke hit a head.

The wind is moaning? Aye my love she's not
Cried for just one incident grim as this.
Let me explain. We'd killed one so the lot . . .
Woman! You surprise me! Why such a kiss?

"The wind's proclaiming this settlement
To be a noble one — Paying no rent."

The Craft of Poetry's the Art of War

Attack! Don't think yehr poetry aint war.
Them warbling noises be no kind of birds
They zing — they fly — they smack. They're bullets
And any minute one of them or something
Even rougher on your balls might score.
Put on your hardhat of proletarian scorn;
And when you throw roses — never mind how sweet;
For sweet life's sake don't omit the thorns.

Attack! Those clutching fingers of dawn
Will bundle themselves, soon enough into fists;
Punch you into garbage, put a lid on the can.
You'll get dropped from this or that love-list
By reason of hate — by reason of fear . . . or another:
But if you think this aint war you're dead brother.

Love in the Nineteen Fifties

On that beach with light shifting breaths
Of breezes touching us like gentle
Curious, strong, all-surrounding presences
Watching, and you watching . . . I stuck a gull's
Tailfeather askew ten white degrees
Out of perpendicular to match
The slant of the nearest sail on that diseased
Warm doubt of a day.

                            Grief hope and fury
Were all there, speaking tentatively
In a jury just met.

                         Wants too early
Stirring your blood, vision, nerves and mine
Over that tilting token in the sand;
Having made a sign, still wanted a sign
While low lightblue waves just tapped the island.

        IN THAT TIME THE WISE
        RARELY SWORE TO ANYTHING
        SINCE MOST WORDS WERE LIES

Dig Up My Heart

Dig up my heart from under Wounded Knee
Where it's been living as a root in the ground
Whispering the beat, to fool mine-detectors.
Though there may not be much Indian in me
That fraction was here first. It's senior
Take this heart to grow a man around.

I shall be Heartman — All heartmuscle!
Strong and of longest endurance
I've acted, thought and dreamt to nurse my will
Proud for the day of the People's Judgement
When vision rides again and all that's meant
Is said and flashed from eyes once thought blind.
Fewer and fewer of us, rest now in silence.

The Minor Poet With the Major Voice

His larynx like a rattle on a stick
This minor poet with a major voice
Shakes it at us . . . buttocks, neck and head
We're flailed from texts all titled with choice
Erectile and/or head-hanging puns. "You
Whimper-wicked, bedamned and bedamning
Moralists!" He cries. We droop limp and blue
With anguish for every uncommitted sin
Knowing few stranger loves than this sense-dumb
Clown reactionary, easy to keep in hand
Ape-conscientious, homo sapient cerebrumed whim
Of-a-god's creature! Watch now while he expands
With hailstorm-windy-whip words (Applause!) Tall
Thunderhead going to flash, gush and fall . . .

The Stormbirds

In a storm the dull gulls flock inland.
The tern, the gallant tern makes out to sea;
Tacking, slanting against a thirty-knot wind
To where the action is, and plumb shifts
Like hands of a clock with springs gone wild;
Fishing at their best where nothing stays pinned;
Swirling in flocks like snow upon green drifts:
Like a mind never at rest, they are at rest.

Realisant souls are the souls solidly
Set in these unsolid worlds and spaces.
With everything restless, nothing staying just so;
I keep in this eternal state of fission:
Back from a mission, off towards a mission;
Simultaneously I return and go.

To a Goddam Boss

You proffered me soft compliments when my hand was out
    for cash . . .
After all, the workers' due . . . We can't live on air.
Then you looked at me with a musing stare
Saying, "Milt, why be so rash?
This world's not going to crash.
Why not stick to your lovely love poems
Which would be welcome in the proudest homes?
The trouble with you's you don't just jibe — you slash."

If your system was so secure, why were you afraid?
Asking for a gentler social criticism?
Today, as for essentials, I've got it made;
Don't bother coming back with your sad wisdom.
How can you buy me now in these times when it's sung
How I ripped lyric fragments from the devil's bloody tongue?

Begging Pardon of that Other Milton and Others

Oh Thou Who maketh herbage rise
The bull to shit and fertilize
Must you let it spray over absolutely everyone?
So we're undone, completely caked with it?

But then I think, like our renowned Premier;
The Universe is evolving as it should . . .
Struck dumb by such awful profundity
I muse . . . How could poets exist
Without a plentiful supply of bullshit?
Not to eat, as that revered nutritionist
Has advised, upstaging Marie Antoinette:
But to scrape and flay, calling the stuff
By its rightful name. But alas, most of us
Fear doing that. Instead spread more of it.

Impatience to prevent that murmur, cries:
I'll do it! Chew it to the last dumb twit!
If poetry-persons think that it's wise
To be stupid, telling stupid lies
Til they've reduced themselves to half-wits,
Then they're part of the predatory scene
In which I — The predators' predator
Rage cyclonic . . . An enthralled destroyer.
Their bullshit serves to make the grass grow green.

The Aim of Life is Life

(*from several sources, scientific, traditional
and literary: this poem is mainly for one I've
named 'The Blot'*)

Since you lunged thru danger, taking my arm
To pull me away from my chosen death,
Your life and its quality became my charm;
Marking my deeds with yours, breath by breath.

Life is fire controlled. Best when it understands
It burns and festers death; with hands
Which flame easiest lighting other brands.

Now you sicken and it's I who pursue.
First it was my mother who bore me
Then you forced my continuity.
To make a truth of mine, your own life's got to be true.
I leak mad liver oil — it's good for you.
Come on . . . Open wide and drink this brew.

! Use the Whole Environment for a Medium !

Like a fighter, face one callous from blows:
When his very calves jump with shocking force
     into his knuckles;
He knows he's won a prize, a good blow . . .
Whether he wins or loses, a good blow:
So it is with me when I've written a poem
Though all the Romes and would-be Romes still stand
Voila! Regard this fine stone I've thrown!

! USE THE WHOLE ENVIRONMENT FOR A MEDIUM !
Don't let it clobber you or choke
From weary grief the words back down your throat.
Those beauties you see are for celebration.
These agonies, insults and injuries —
You must curse or else be stoppered dumb.

No Music From the Bar

No music from the bar. Damn Sunday
When no stripper wags her miscellaneous cuts
Of long pig, grotesquely meaning to look horney;
No singer whines impressions of a Yank in rut
Dripping polluted tears for damn dead Dixie:
Or Continentalist band beats and blares
You deaf, for what's meant to be eternity.

Idiotic noise, transmogrified to music
Or something like that, in my muffled room upstairs
Blurred me til I slept like a mosquito
Insentient to the worse civic bedlam —
Not quite serene: But now, fixed to this bed of fright
Through churning Sunday night in the volcano
Of a cannonading city; I'm frigged —
With no note to play against metallic discord
Short of getting up and making rage my lord . . .
Sleepless in Toronto — home of the homesick.

Sonnet Written Coldly Lest I Cry

I speak this bit with this tongue cut from steel
(drunk when I got the news, I cried then)
That this skull-locked computer prints — *"treason"* . . .

A land is often likened to a woman . . .
A nation a man? That image seems unreal.
Absurd as well, you say, to sign a poem
With no name other than a land and people?
It's those of our wants which are hard to cohere
Pump room from poetic lungs to set homes
Where unslaked words are needed sure as mortar;
Which greed and ego, for their lives, must break,
Letting nothing exist except for their sake.

I'm speaking of the murder of Pat Lowther.
Those who were mistaken, make no mistake.

For Mao and Others

The old guy gets older . . . Accent more pronounced;
Sometimes only friends can understand him.
Is it senility or is it wisdom?
 Quoting old, hard-learned, but also new axioms
He still moves easy with the Earth's spin
Recognized, taken into account.
Some say he's getting crazy like a fox —
Shouts at the morning as if he'd just been born.

"How are things today?" he asks; not "How are you?"
"What time is it?" "What's the date?" "What year?"
Then with a glint of pride and note of warning
*"Have you justified your existence yet, this morning?"**
He won't be balked, waits with a nagging ear.
His second highest praise: "Me son; that's real sincere . . . "

*The folk-wisdom of the Maritime working people is just too profound
for academicians to really record. It shocks them silly. The line quoted is
actually a Maritime folk-saying.

40

Aurora Borealis

Quetzecoatl: Big befeathered worm
Trapped between emptiness and atmosphere —
Void he can't breathe, air whose flavour
He can't stand — it's not quite right — squirms
From horizon to horizon, all night
While stars like needles impudently pierce him.

What a God! And what a coat he's got!
What shall I tell, and will I tell who what?
His feathers live as he does, swarm
Curling and uncurling, knotting and unknotting
Over that mightily bright, non-dazzling form.
Heard like modulated small winds in a pine-thicket
Within my lusting-to-comprehend head,
For no air-sound brooms it this far down
A whole gang of fiddlers is jazzing
Tunes like stroking fine cloth on fur.

Come ye faithful . . . Come ye faithless ones
To see this poet writhing, glad and half-crazy
Overseas, overland, overhead skyline to skyline . . .

"The Fascists are Coming!
The Fascists are Coming!"

(THIS MACHINE KILLS FASCISTS . . .
Sticker on Woody Guthrie's guitar)

"The Fascists are coming! The Fascists are coming!"
Well here I'm waiting with this machine-gun —
Ideological, figurative: but it can pin
As many poppies to as many foul torsos
As its other mechanical twin.
Once we've supplemented spirit with matter
To what a daisy-picking we'll go . . .

Shoot to wound if possible because a corpse
Can't be insulted when we curse it in French.
Supposing curses are all the French we know
Use those for a start. Can you imagine the wrench
Of futile rage that Fascist will get with the blow
Sincerely intended to knock him into sense?

Hard On

Flag tall in my wind. Juju man
Symbol of me! Up you stare when I'm proud,
One-eyed, curious at the froth of heaven.
Many times you've stood and crowed aloud
Then lain stubbornly limp when I was shamed.
Don't, by me or anyone, count yourself blamed
For if I lost you, you'd sure be missed;
Though there are fools (I swear!) who regret you exist.

Look at that woman, tall, head-high like you:
When I think of her in the levelest
Terms, reverently counting her virtues,
Unselfishly I think of you too. Fine lust
Which swings my craning mind to the bare facts;
Making my fellow-person real — not abstract!

Island Moon

The moon's a dime worn out of round;
Clear stare from a one-eyed captain's tomcat;
Fountain spraying with clear hard pale cider
This rolling land with half-abandoned orchards
Too small today to be kept for sound
Countable profit, culled for other rewards.

Who has named these colours of the moon;
Given to this pasture, that oatfield, those slight
Poplars like shivering-on-one-leg sentries
With short tartans wrapped round them tight?
The road down to the untraceably gone shipyard
Was dug deep once to make do for a trench;
And the river's glittering like a silver fork
Once stuck hard in the land, hefted and bent.

Senator Ozymandias

A quarterer back-and-forth of this land
Says: "One place where you could die of thirst; stone
Grapples up to mountains, dry as the sand
Wind-carved to mad shapes that do seem to frown
At me hiking to my own sweet command
And my water-bottle's. By God I read
Freshly painted, black on white, among things
Plain valueless — NO TRESPASSING! Who fed
Ego in his guts making *that* appear
Where the hopefulest of money-kings
Would find no workable ore, just despair?"
(nothing progressed there, not even decay)
"Some Yank's been here!" Rage rose hot red and bare
As his axe came up to smash it away.

A Theory of Bushmen

"The stronger the beast: the stronger the dream"
Those Kalahari Bushman theorize.
Enraptured speech which is never dogmatic
Takes them like a song. A shift in the gleam
Of one's eyes, incarnates a speaker
Walking months away — feathering down time.

The rich man's dream, flared onto retinas
Bawled in variant tones, each chord louder;
Dazzles and hoots to shock from us
Our own visions as possessing demons . . .
Not like the dreams of lions and elephants
Flowering from the earth of our own souls.
New colours to our fires spurt from those coals.

Of Time and the Fighter

"What time is it?" I'm asked. I ask "Where?"
"Here. Where else?" I'm answered. I ask, "When?"
(I ought to tell you I'm a historian —
Amateur of course, but better than many.
(Who's better than me? I can't think of any.
Others of course, possess other qualities)
But my questioner stops still to stare
Or, more often, moves off hurriedly.

I can't help it. I'm so magnetic
Any watch I wear — even those advertised
As demagnitized, stops in about a week
And anyway I measure time by microseconds
In a fight — or else by centuries
(I've got to tell you this) also in a fight.

The Wake-Up Raven

A most unghostly whistle, like a toy
Factory's — at the dim brown hour of four
Angled down from those ponderously stirred
Trees near the heaving, hunching slowpoke waves;
Used to shake me quick from dreams to wonder:
Til I knew it had to be a raven
Waking his relatives to plunder
Breakfast in this first, best, worst hour of war.

Now it's all routine, I'm up and to work
At a craft not the canniest raven knows
With half an ear for panic in the forest
Where they as well raise hell and drive blows.
Such quirks in my beloved reality:
The cruelest time for raven-work's best for me.

There Blows a Man

Face brooding, changing like a clouded sky
Dark with grim thought, and with lips
Perpetually twisting for a word
That can't get out — so stubborn the jaw grips
His coiled brain's exit. There's drama
In this shaggy, blackbearded bum. I've wondered
What he's up to, thinks he's up to, would be up to
When he makes crude drawings alongside cruder verse.

What can I say?
                    He should be more than he
Is, his dreams roll more. Red flame ought to
Run from his nostrils, smoke curl up from his eyes
And when he speaks it shouldn't be idiocy
Such as might be piped by a passed pawn
Whose master weighs sacrifice.
                        Somewhere a lion yawns.

Turn About is Fair Play

Don't look at me, you woman damning sexism,
My broad shoulders, flame curling from my eyes;
Pretty and neat carpenteering hands . . .
My able arms — don't dare imagine them hugging
Or I'll return the compliment likewise
And look with lust on you as you do at me.

In my grey-green checked tweed suit don't I look
With sandy hair and contrasting white beard,
Enough for any lass to pillow dreams on?
But don't dare mess me with such sexist muck
For I am human too, not just a good fuck.
Did I ever say that's all you were?
If I ain't only that, you ain't either;
But let me praise you sexually, sometimes for luck.

Drunk Thoughts of Bethune

With the second beer my wits return . . .
At number three they're holding steady.
Now to nurse my way through number four and all.
Such is the life of a controlled alcoholic.
Colours are more percepted. We see the shabby
State of being in this fort of commerce
Producing such natures as this which burns me
As all men burn, normally more happily;
Though normal pushes ahead of the usual.
Take for instance our Norm. He was normal
Though he's half-made-out a mad hero
Fighting to the death at war with death
Or Fascism . . . The principle's the same
As Continentalism — all those thieving games.
Our kind are moths, tongueing the big red flame
By which we're consumed. But, then who's not?
This fuse will burn. The question is where to?
I envy him.
                    Waiter! Cut me off!
They never do it when you tell them to . . .

The Game of Cards

The King? That's a proud one . . . but can be trumped.
The Queen and Jack make fireworks running loose
Through a poor pack just counted as numbers
Til spirits wane, lusting for a wild deuce.
What will it profit you to flash and thump
At your game? Which is an obvious blunder?

These hands are two of many, and shuffle
Such a host of faces, souls, powers being unsealed,
I plot through centuries as if they were hours;
Minutes my markers for millenia.
All this makes for one delightful scuffle;
So you oughtn't to think me impersonal
When in plain sight and all proof to all
Who have denied it all, I play the Ace of Truth.

The Man From Headless Valley

He was blocky and taller than you'd take him to be at first. Had a way sometimes of being so quiet that, if there were three or four other people around, you wouldn't realize at first that he was there. That's how I met him first. I'd stepped into the tavern at a place called None-Of-Your-Business and was looking for a friend — not one particular friend, just any friend — looked around twice, noticing in particular every person in the place . . . seeing no friend; and the third time I looked around here was this man who I'd never noticed, and he was looking at me.

He looked away, not nervously or guiltily, just politely. But something had come over me. I wanted to sit with him. I walked over to him, inclined my head toward one of the empty chairs; he nodded assent and I sat down. Then it is, in the usual case, that each man sits there half-ignoring the other til the tension gets too high for one of them and he has to speak. Only it was different here. There was no tension. I'm sure the quietness I felt flowed out from him. His relaxation was fantastic but I could swear he was completely alert. As for me the nervous tension — something you'd call loneliness but wasn't really that — which had been consuming me when I'd entered the tavern, went away. I realized I was tired, but it was a pleasant tiredness. I think I actually dozed. Then I started a bit; thought maybe I was being rude: I took out a pack and offered him an Export — not saying a word. He accepted with a smile. (His face glowed — it was startling) then took a pipe out of his pocket, broke up the cigarette and stuffed it into the bowl, paper and all. It was only then I noticed he was an Indian . . . He wore some sort of soft-tanned jacket, with fringes, true, but that meant nothing. I guess it was the old-fashioned peaked cap, quite new, which threw me off. As for his colour; I'm black Irish and he was lighter than me if anything. His cheekbones were only moderately high on his square face. He could have called himself anything, except maybe something like a Swede or a Biafran, and got no argument.

His eyes, however, were black as sin; they looked at me and were completely merry, though no expression showed in his facial muscles.

"Are you going to ask me where I'm from?"

"Why, no, but, now that you mention it, where are you from?"

"I'm from Headless Valley — born there!"

I had heard the story, or if you will the Legend of Headless Valley — How it got its name. But if I disbelieved him I didn't show it. I was too curious.

"Isn't there another name for the valley? Indian? The *Wa* — No, if you came from there you'd call it another name still . . . ?

"We call it Headless Valley. We say it in English."

"Yes — But how do you know English? I mean, you're here; you came out, but how do your people know — ?

"I'm here. You can seem me. I told you. How many other people do you think there are who you didn't see? Who didn't tell you?"

I felt an urge to scratch my head. "You, friend, if I may quote Confucius, are getting more and more confusing all the time . . . " I also was thinking that, if English was not his mother tongue (had he implied that or had he implied the opposite? he'd implied both it and the opposite at the same time) then he must have learned his English in school. He did not make his larynx rattle and roar, Hollywood-Red-Man style; he didn't speak extremely softly and with extreme care to distinguish between fact and opinion like another type of Indian accent unnoticed by Hollywood. He spoke perfect English like a graduate of Moscow University might speak perfect English — except he didn't say 'whom' — and that, after all, is a pedantry. His only Indian mannerism was the way he used his eyes. He punctuated with his eyes.

I had to change the subject. We talked a while of other things while the whole business stewed at the back of my mind. Finally I asked — in the middle of talking about something else; "What do your people call yourselves?"

"The Headless People," he said. I laughed.

"It's not a joke — though maybe it was in the first place," he said, "You know how many Indian tribes are called by names originally given them by their enemies — instead of their own names for themselves? Well, we changed that . . . We call ourselves after our enemies — in gratitude to them for giving up their heads, and for our own heroes . . ."

I still thought he was joking; but anyway he was some story-teller. "Yes," I said, "I know that's why they call it 'Headless Valley'; because travellers who go too far into it are usually found lying around somewhere without their heads. I guess you're a pretty warlike bunch of people?"

Then his eyes lit up as if they could have burned me down on the spot. His voice went down to a conventional Indian rumble, like he was an old car and there was something wrong with the muffler. "Warlike — No. And if the word you mean is 'murderous' it isn't murder either."

"Then how . . . ?"

"I'll tell you — White Man . . . You didn't tell me your name?"

Frank."

"Hello Frank, I'm Earnest." He held out his hand and we shook. I was careful not to laugh til after . . .

"Frank and Earnest!"

He grinned. "Well any white man's name can do for my white name — And my Indian name I'm not allowed to tell you . . .

"I'll tell you: we've got to keep that valley closed. It's all right for us to know about the White Man; but the White Man mustn't know about us. We don't want interference. It seems to be the White Man's national sport. Sometimes he interferes for profit, sometimes for religion; but if he can get neither profit or religious benefit from interference he interferes just the same — just for the sake of interference. Interference hurts the Indian . . . And when the White Man sees the Indian has been hurt by his interference he uses that as an excuse for more interference. So we don't want interference. Just the same we don't want to be unfriendly. When someone comes into our valley and finds us, we meet him in a friendly way . . . "

"What if he's heard about the legend? Wouldn't he be suspicious?"

"Yes . . . They're usually suspicious at first. But we win them over."

"And then you cut off their heads?"

"No . . . They cut off their own heads!"

Strange as this may seem to you, it was getting almost impossible for me to disbelieve the man now. I felt chills going through my lower body; around the groin as they will go at moments like that. I practically started twitching in my chair, stretching my neck in odd positions; mentally twisting my elbows, hands and wrists into positions even odder . . .

"How's that managed?" I asked finally.

"Oh, some of our boys are pretty handy," was his answer. "We manage to rig something up out of the materials at hand."

"That wasn't what I meant — " I said, beginning to get a little saner — though as a matter of fact it had been what I meant.

"We entertain them — all in a friendly way. We give them whiskey. We keep a stock on hand; though we don't drink it ourselves except on special occasions . . . "

I began to force myself to laugh again. *Whiskey!*

"We put something in it!" He was completely serious, not a trace of mirth in his eyes. He said some Indian word and then began to translate "*Psycho-*" It was not an expression he was familiar with . . .

"A psychedelic drug — " I offered . . .

"Yes . . . And it makes them very friendly; very conscious of our problem when we explain it to them."

"In a friendly way!" I said. Migod it could work! It was conceivable. I had seen friends of mine in the grips of a psychedelic drug who hardly knew they existed; though their minds remained perfectly clear in other ways. I even knew a case when a guy, high on LSD, had become aware of the problem of the bourgeois class — and decided to lessen it by shooting the first bourgeois he could find to aim a gun at; which happened to be himself . . .

I looked at him, completely believing, and I swear I don't know whether I said the next word, thought it out loud, or he read my thought and answered it:

"Murder!" was the word.

"No — It's not murder . . . It isn't even war," he said. "Mister; we're Indians of the old religion. We live on animals and we don't murder *them* either. We pray to the animals to come within range and offer up their bodies — And if all goes well, if we're living right, they do. Just the same we not only pray to our white visitors to die so as to keep our secret; we ask them right to their faces. Besides it's not murder when you kill animals, because animals have no existential sense of death. Neither have the white people any existential sense when we ask them."

"Existential?" I said — surprised at him using the word.

"I'm a graduate of the University of British Columbia," he explained, "I have a lot of time outside; logging, fishing, things like that and things not like that. Look . . . "

He opened his coat and showed the medals pinned to his shirt. He had fought in Korea.

"I know what you're thinking," he said. "That was stupid. But I never found out til after I was there . . . and I thought I should do something for the White people; like fighting their enemies."

"I think you were fighting *for* our enemies . . . "

"I came to think so myself."

There followed a silence while each of us examined our beer and drank it, bubbles and all. As belief declined and disbelief came creeping in; I had a thought —

"Listen," I said, "there's a flaw in your story. I know you get them in a state where they're not scared to cut off their own heads — but what if they don't *want* to cut off their heads? Scared or fearless or not?"

"Then one of our people, as a token of sincerity, to show that it's all in friendship — "

"Will cut off his own head!" I exclaimed.

"Not his — hers!" he said. "Women do it!" And I tell you he was crying, just for a moment . . .

"You know," he went on rapidly, "we've done what all Indians should do — what the most successful do. We've adapted to the White Man's ways . . . Learned the most useful of his customs; but learned to use them in an Indian way: and kept our independence."

"What did you take your degree in?"

"Anthropology . . . "

The Game of Snooker

When I've set my cue to take aim
And seen it's gauged dead-on, right-off;
Not to fear this sure life's kiss of a moment
And shoot not too hard, not too soft
Has so many analogies in the flame
I carry about from lights-on to lights-off:
I leave it to you, imperishable listener
Lusting for strong words . . . also fearing them
To lengthen this sonnet into the stances
Of figures round the table, lay of the balls
Each with its colour and significance
Of where it's placed in relationship to all
The rest, the pockets of success or less . . .
And speaking of the rest: What realizations
Have those others, each with his wand?
Such things decide the fates of men and
Worlds, discrepancies, unities and/or nations.

The Stratford Swan

That awful day I saw a Stratford Swan:
First time in my life . . . Bright she was
(the day, not the swan — it was neuter;
for all an eye could tell clipped from porcelain
in its muddy phase, with a cookie cutter)
When the knowledge hit that only its wings were clipped:
That grace unzipped: its pride in white flown;
I spluttered a curse to flutter in his cause.

"Eleventh province with your roadsigns in code
To fool invading Yankees long ago;
The Yankees are here, and what's worse
You're here to build blunt fronts concealing mazes . . .
Would it ring a bell or Southern Ontario Ironhead
To yell: "SWANS RETURN WHERE THEY'RE FED!"

The Chinook Bow

Should I wish for ignorance? Not to know
It's the curvature of the Earth showing
When I see that broad bow of a cloud bending
White with a faint blend of yellow
Across the whole pale blue undrinkable
Width of a sky like weird Homeric wine
Tempting the throat and tongue
To drink for all time, not getting too drunk?
Or want to see Uncle God grunting to pull
That bow proud with helpfulness to send
This chinook, crooning low along the land
To blow warmth into the gut of winter?
Should I want to sink back to an age
Where innocent visions glowed grand
As they were unfulfilable? Hell no . . . But
Would it be all wrong
To balance on that bridge, dreaming this windsong?

Mon Ami Jacques

Mon ami Jacques? If he laid down he'd die.
It's been about to happen since we two
Met in a dream, parted with a low cry.
Only anguish keeps him alive.
His people suffer, so he continues . . .

Now he's further abused with a great bribe.
To throw his poor worn soul in the garbage.
Murder, unlike suicide, is forgiveable.
Rich men's voices crack like ribs, with fear
Since pain-honed wits gained his enraged piece
A square on the board from which to attack . . .
But does his shadow know how tired he is?
If he takes their gifts he won't last one year.

Mon ami Jacques: Though even a swallow
May find a spot in a crumbling river bank
To dig like a mole, rest in his own burrow;
The place for you isn't one of refuge.
Count the odds as chances . . . Look! They're huge!
Do not crawl into any other man's hole.

In Memory of Joe En Lai

1898-1976
(*the chinese* 'chou' *is pronounced* 'joe')

Never close the door on a parting friend.
Most inauspicious — that: hinting an end.
Watch him clear as he goes down the lane;
Photons from your eyes like a rain
Of blessings and good wishes. Hum
And memorize a song in his name
Which you'll hold secret til he comes again.

Never give a sign it's over and done.
Greet every new friend partly for his sake;
Thinking of him as just now gone and due back soon;
And if he doesn't return let loose that tune
To find and call him back wherever he's run.
Remember him behind in time, dream of him ahead.
Follow these instructions — even if he's dead.

Auntie Continental

To the Void with the Continent! Cut it loose!
What does it think it is? Some kind of planet?
Heave-ho! Boost it to the Asteroids . . .
If bedbugs shine, she'll still be blocking views
But that's the look-out of those silly lookouts
Who've thrown their own good eyes away
For glasses manufactured in the U.S.A.
Don't let the creature starve. Ration it
To all that's foul and seeps from haemorrhoids
Swear this and raise our mugs of hearts ferment
To Canada and the World;
Brim-level til every hair's curled.
The point is justice. Fear to let it bend.

The Devil's sick and swears he'll be a monk
In the wee parish of Saint James Carter;
On Earth, of Sol, Galaxy, Universe.
If he gets well there'll be some deviltry
Near the Great Red Spot of Jupiter.
Find the rural route by the smell of skunk.

The Carter Imperium

The Emperor announces his conversion.
Christ Crucified, as in that time before
Now's the proudest trophy flaunted by reshuffling corps
In maneuvers of consolidation
While fools hurrah, perceiving dissolution.
Tom Pariah knocks, and is received
For the looks of it, awaiting the vote.
With the balloteers again deceived
His poor old black arse exits by a rude boot.
Scientific masques announce with ho-hums:
All men are robots, programed by their genes.
Speak, for yourself, before the stop-watch clicks!
You are the robots, and the junkman comes.

Poem Beginning
With A Quote from Heracleitus

"Struggle is the mother of all things"
You ask me why I write to make enemies:
Your answer is I do it deliberately;
He who makes no enemies wins no friends.
Struggling we rose from beasts to human beings:
Struggle in the end makes us more human;
When there's no more struggling, life ends.

Struggle, Mother Struggle, I'll never be weaned
Of this passion sucked from your strong tits.*
Uprising shone-through sculpture-clouds, my dreams
Meet contrary draughts, churn into winds of wit.
My lifepulse moves in waves to hit rocks,
Ebb back, replenish, come on for more shocks.

*After much inner struggle, I decided to dispense with the
nicety-orthodox spelling of 'tits' as 'teats' — the pronunciation is
'tits' anyhow . . . .

Letter to My Redheaded Son

Young maple leaves, copper with a delicate flush,
are taut and hardly bent by the limb-twist breeze;
I'm repenetrated by delight that made you
And makes fool poets call the spring green.

Their budded shapes, nearly stiff assagais
are held so long as sun and wind engage
in the see-saw battle with the Ice Age
which is spring here.
                            No advantage
this or that color might earn
isn't borne bleeding into the kaleidoscope.
Suicide to step here, with no charge of hope.

Still you hear poets calling the spring green
in air-currents which bluff, whine and churn
under the corn-silk lashes of the sun.
Life is fine to talk of. Living must learn
to fight — (no civil marriage in those days)
You know your name, my son. The truth is it's mine.

Shoot Yourself or Shit Yourself

Shoot yourself or shit yourself, Friar Northbush;
Taking bad aim, missing that vital part.
Wanting you alive to see you flush
With urgency I urge you, try for the heart . . .
You must be a marksman to hit there —
So small it could merely be brushed aside
With such obfuscation you aired
Your vocal apparatus — no one could say you lied.

Now look at you! Only a Canadian!
Any Yankee Ph(oney D(octor outranks you
Who would'ev dressed us all True Tory Blue
Masqued goalies waving archetypal symbols —
No forwards allowed, and no defencemen —
Manipulated spotlight for a puck.
Since you set those lesser rules, who's to blame
That even meaner promoters claim the game;
Ousting your Loonie Line to put in idiots?

Take heart! Their aim's the same — negation
For cause of class, all which motivates
Poets to soar and swoop enraged
Spraying antifreeze to kill or cure —
Sweet notes and sour likewise skewering
You who nurse the half-life of this cruel age.
Whatever you do don't try for the bunghole.
A bullet in a horse's arse could be fatal.

Celebrate the Battle of the Little Big Horn

Celebrate the Battle Of The Little Big Horn
On each unwholesome century-mark
Of that public-relations nation born
Promising all men would be free and equal
For it will also be a hundredth year
Since Crazy Horse, Sitting Bull, Rain-in-the-Face
With Man Whose Very Horses Inspire Fear
Plus many more braves from many brave tribes
Stomped their first centennial down in disgrace.

Ask this American Earth, "Where are your children?"
Ask Hesperus, "How many would be fair?"
No nation this side of the Ocean
Has any claim at all til this matter
Of injustice those Old Reds fought against —
Mainly to start a new tradition,
Is settled in a way fit for celebration;
Since, Spring, Summer, Fall and Winter all are stolen.

Dance proud for mean death at The Little Big Horn
To George Armstrong Custer, called Woman Killer
Not for performance with his little wee horn;
For those enemies he preferred to warriors
On the Wachita where he left men to die
Within gunshot and the sight of smoke . . . earshot of
                                                    their cries.

At Levis Where the Current Meets the Tide

At Levis where the current meets the tide;
Beneath Quebec's rammed face — crowned for relief . . .
Walls built to top a wall . . . What's the idea?
Waves heave, hump and fall like grappling wrestlers
With sweat for jerseys. Which ones take our side —
Or should Atlantic folk hold anyone's brief?

Seawinds bluster up. Landbreeze flushes down.
Pink and blue flags point where they've just been flung.
What's the time? I've worn no watch since thirty —
Swore off ageing, watching the world grow young.
Cut us off from Ontario? Here's some news!
Say it again. She sounds too sweet for truth.
Without a sheen of salt, my face feels dirty.

A WINNING YOUNG LAD OF CAN-PO
URGENTLY WANTING TO GO
SAID, "I'LL BE A POET
SO NO ONE WILL KNOW IF
MY CLAIMS ARE FALLACIOUS OR SO . . . . "

With an undeveloped smirk of talent
Promising decade after decade
Like a Liberal or P.C. politican
Tucked and hauled in Yankee baggage;
By a parasitic flair for academic intrigue
This professor in the Chair of Boredom
Gets announced, pronounced, loud-hailed a big
Bull poet.
                No craft, love, imagery or rage
Can this one prove.
                    God weight my foot to crush
Even this drab fool who must be stepped on
For fear youth pukes at verse, force-fed the mush
Of this grass-hopping, fake also-ran;
Who'll die just as he lives:
                    A promising young man.

Two Buzzards Came Down

Two buzzards came down. Was this a sign?
I'd lain so still so long they'd thought me dead;
Thinking thoughts the like of which I'd often condemned
With the compass of my body turned to enthuse
My enemies and confuse my friends.
                                            Bemused
But unamused, accused of not using my views
To fuse with signals from afar, without news
That could fool a child or a Marxist.
                                            Defused
I lay when dried-blood-mixed-with-phlegm coloured
Wings zipped shadows clipping my newly ancient head;
Sweeping my grassy mattress like lawnmowers.

Then did the red cells bobbling through my blood
Yell out, "We're made of iron — not lead!"
Those vultures shivered : Slick as boomerangs
Fled as from the grabs of orang-utangs;
Having seen those fateful signs of life
My critics notice to their grief and dread.

U.F.O.

Shall I compare you to a U.F.O?
You're just as mysterious.
Shall I compare a U.F.O. to you?
Those vehicles exist. I saw one sure
As the fact you're gone and I've tried
Hate as a cure for love
In covens of thorn with roses, where I hide
From complicated beauty more like yours;
Rating my half-cut death as fate
When I'd promised fate more future than that.

It shone like the sun: but only for an eye
Which sought it out; otherwise just a strange
Moveable star it was. Nor did it glare
Or illuminate the scene around it.
Until my look fitted onto that stare
Winter had combined all other seasons.
On other planets other things change
And I'd loved you too long, at most for half a reason

The Pipe-Dottler

I wouldn't learn the art . . . the whole of it;
Only wanting craft enough to get through
This waiting time, to what I was really up to.
Knowing my mood to the last wart and tit
The captain persisted "Look at that . . . Think on this!
Listen Sonny: There's a lot you'll miss
In that dream-life you hope will come true
As did we all. And should that fate
You're climbing hard to catch, catch you:
You'll be wishing back on this — somewhat late."

He dottled his pipe. "Look you! I was told
Much similar things . . . Paid small attention.
You count my life success? Hell man I curse
Myself at bedtime like a mad old convert;
Because it's won — That old ambition's done.
What's coming next to task the good old horse?
I don't . . . I wish . . . Kid: What might you ask?"

The Waterhole

(for Moritz Sussholz)

Here is the waterhole. Here are the Jews.
Here are the Arabs on the other side.
What are the rules for this? A duel
With thirsty death the consolation prize?
The front is quiet as an old scarred sphinx;
Strategy looks elsewhere. Warriors dream
Of metaphysically tall cool drinks.
Nightly parties from each combat team
Go down to drink, fill, and fetch;
Saying when they meet, *"Salaam!" "Sholom!"*
Christ don't they know there's a war on?
Christ, Allah and Jehovah should be there to listen
To the quiet, intense arguments
Of those able to curse, and bless in each idiom.

Full Moon Soliloquy

Moon, queen of the tides and blood and me:
You're full tonight and I feel chunks of fury
Rattling about like meteors in my brainpan.
Which is prophecy, which vision memory
I hardly know or want to define.
If the past is dead, the future's buried with it.
This fist rising now will never slam down;
The moon never set . . . no more work for poets.

Last night I asked you to read me a bold
Scribble of yours, long part of my strength.
You said, "That poem's forty years old!"
Listen, old son, if it ever had significance
It has that now, and will have for ages.
The higher comes the moon, higher my thoughts rage.

To Joe's Last Grunt

Joseph, you're mistaken. It's not me
Who's the god of your mumbling, muttering
Curses at mixed-up totality. You only see
A humbly proud, proudly humble . . .

Only?

Did I say *only?* What sort of stuttering
Foul fluttering, gutter-plucked puttering
Word was that? Don't you call me *only!*

I'm a man. Whether calm or furious
These curious sounds I make are human words —
Though some say "human" to mean "less than human".
If you're worried by what I've said and done
To bother, itch and nag you with optimism;
Don't try to put me down. Haul down the Sun . . .

Our True/False National Anthem

Oh Canada or home and native land
Such awe and reverence do those Yanks command!
Champions of liberty of their own brand . . .
Their liberty to take us all in hand.
Proudly we mock the United Nations now
That not every vote goes the American way;
We masters of the Canadian bow
Backs turned and arse up to the U.S.A.

Oh Canada beneath whose shining skies
A Yankee deproduction line runs south.
If we don't stop it — it won't be stopped.
What curses will our sons and daughters mouth
When cheated before they drew a breath, they stare
At Canada, the cruel north stripped stark bare?

There's a Cookoo in the Nest

There's a joker in the deck. But who
It is seems doubtful — he's made so confused
All this zealous, determined gang . . .
Errors and sabotage collide. Blame zooms
Round and about like an enraged boomerang,
Threatening to scatter the whole crew.

There's a cookoo in the nest. Things will be
Bad until he's grown for identification . . .
When he could be hailed as the almighty
Committer of needed purifications.
I warn you this can happen. Such things do.

Pigs

Truck's painted red, sun yellow, pigs quite pink
From sunburn — I wouldn't be surprised:
It being precious little they get
Of wind and sun. Now here's this jolly trip.
Never mind . . They don't feel burnt yet
And never will — the way things are set.

So far they've been well kept by the man;
Confined, but otherwise done much good by
Nourishing meals, delivered right on time.
Now comes this surprise . . . A world to scan
While they zip through it. There's another sky
Higher and brighter than above their pen.

Filling their eyes with nearness and distance;
Two of them stand up, almost like men —
Balancing by forelegs on top of the cab;
Like the Cabot Brothers, gazing wide ahead.
It's for this they were bred, born, doctored, fed.

Sonnet of the Most Unthought Thought of Mao

INDIVIDUALITY . . . YES! INDIVIDUALISM . . .
   NO!
If your head had size and mass like the Earth's
With an iron core as Earth has —
                       Although
It would be sweaty work with my six-inch chisel
Still I'd bore this axiom into you
Til bone split and brow profoundly wrinkles . . .
                         "SO?"

Draegermen, *activists in underground rescue,*
particularly in mine disasters, are not so
much professionals as players at a dangerous
hobby. Certainly strong individuals, since
their art is for the good of humankind; they
are not individualists.

Clouds lean low to spit sleet in my eyes
While the panic shrill of new-found convictions
Afraid of doubt as they once feared the devil
Swirls every rag about.
Ban knowledge of one notion
Where everything is in some aspect so
And you'll get colour-blind, deafer to my shout:
"INDIVIDUALITY . . . YES! INDIVIDUALISM . . .
   NO!"

Love of the World

I lived a long time with a bitter girl;
Longer than with any other lover.
When she looked at other ones she snarled
As I said, "Love me — Love my world!"

When I made a comment on another
She rampantly refused to see my humour.
Her eyes curled with the burning smokes of Hell
As I said, "Love me — Love my world!"

It's true, *p'tit'*, that this dung-enriched
Ball of slag we live on, is badly used
By the gardeners shucking off their wits;
But hatred must be spare, applied with care.
Commence your love, my love, by being amused.

She made love furious as if it was war
Every night, my God, at least twice.
It was work. I tell you. I was sore
When whirling among the fumes of her eyes such lights
Shone soft towards me; I was rewarded;
Still catechizing: "Love me — Love my world."

On Being Called a Degenerate
by a Magazine Not Called Dead

Now it's degenerate they're calling me
To push me into the circle of
Those whose heads have churned and changed nations.
Bourgeois goofs think it unnatural
That one man can show strong enough
In the wrestle of love and enmity
To rise as seas rise in the worst winds.

Just like the rich, fake proletarians
Who claim that class their property
(What an idea! Such originality!)
Call generative power degeneration
To put on my top mop the same crown
That Mayakovsky and Shelley once owned.

Celebrate Peter the Loggers poem "The Mountain"

(for Pete Trower)

Who else would know and speak so well about
A mountain, as one who's crawled up and all
Round each rock-slide and ferocious redoubt?
Falling to rise again? Rising to fall?
Wrenching ancient conifers from its flanks —
Some excelling thirteen feet through the butt —
By a craft endowed with all except thanks
Eased each down with many's the sure putt?

Finished that godlike labour, should he not
Bow humiliation? Straightaway fly
Out of sight and mind as if he was shot
To that mighty garbagecan in the sky?
"No" he says, not granting even a snort;
Intent on wonders of another sort.

My Life as a Co-Adventurer

"The shares of the carriers (newsboys) is now three and a quarter cents," said the slim young man (even I at twelve recognized him as young) in the starched white shirt and equally neat tie. He pronounced it with all the conviction of a Baptist minister asserting the existence of Hell, only more firmly. After all he had definite evidence.

I'd better go back in this a little.

I've heard that the supreme powers and authorities — right next to God or Satan or whoever it is that rules the world — said at first during the Nova Scotia fisherman's strike that fishermen are co-adventurers; therefore having no right to bargain (uh!) or strike. Then they said and the boat-owners they were backing, subsidizing, and working along with said: the fishermen could join up with a union all right, tho not the kind you'd go looking for. Of course joining an American union usually means you have no right to bargain either.

Now the term co-adventurer is a study in itself. It means that the fisherman goes out on the ocean and stands a good chance of getting into the water. That's an adventure. No doubt about that. It also means the boat-owner stays at home in his office, and stands a good chance of getting into his secretary. That too is undeniably an adventure. Where the term 'adventure' begins to break up, and ought to be replaced by 'disaster', is when the fishermen and the owner begin to divvy up shares. The secretary may not get screwed: but the fisherman certainly will be . . . Many times in the course of a life, or even in the course of a year.

As my knowledge of the joys and woes of a Nova Scotia

fisherman and his employer is practically non-existent; I can only tell of my adventures as another kind of co-adventurer: a weekly newsboy. I know the cream of the newsboys is supposed to be the peddlars of dailies. While the weekly fellows are considered to be practically on vacation. But let me remind you that weekly papers in those days were much heavier than the dailies. Besides the way I sold weekly papers it was work. Not that I'm complaining. I like work. Never minded it. It's bosses I always minded. But peddling weekly papers is a job in which you come in little contact with the boss. Just go down, order the number of papers you think you can sell, plus a few more. Sell them. Go back without your surplus and pay the boss his share. My share was 3 & 3/4 cents out of ten, robbery in the first place. I thought so when I took the job — tho I was only eleven. But for one thing I could stand having the money, and for another it was my father took me down to get the job. I wasn't afraid either of my father's wrath or his fists, though he (lord rest his soul) used them aplenty. I was afraid, however, of appearing wrong in his eyes. Even though, at eleven, I was a good calculator I remained silent when the share was mentioned. In fact I don't think I said one word during the entire interview — my father spoke for me — except to shake hands with the boss and call him "Mr. Marshall." "I'm not Mr. Marshal," he said. "This is H.M. Marshal and Company. I only work here." This did not penetrate. From then on most of the conversation between me and him consisted of me calling him 'Mr. Marshal' and him saying he wasn't 'Mr. Marshal'. Even then I could spot a company man when I saw one. Besides he never did tell what was his name.

Then, in the course of time, 'Mr. Marshal' instructed me in the technique of building a route for the weekly paper (TORONTO STAR WEEKLY it was). I was to knock on doors, introduce myself by name, and say "Do you want to become a regular customer to THE TORONTO STAR WEEKLY?" My Indian blood, which in those days I didn't even know of, nevertheless came to my rescue. My facial muscles didn't twitch, my eyelids didn't even flicker, I said nothing . . . even though the intelligent reader has no doubt detected already that this was a lot of nonsense. I would go to the door, and through knocking (with my fist or on the knocker), by the doorbell, or whatever, *not* introduce myself — who the hell cared whether I was Mickey Acorn or Barnacle Bill The Sailor?) and say: "Do you want to buy THE TORONTO STAR WEEKLY?" If I made a sale, next week I would be back and blandly assume (all this was *not quite* a deliberate con — just the way my mind worked) that the customer had undertaken to buy the Toronto et cetera and so on from me every week. The utter completeness (which in a man would be and is terrifying — I smile like a tiger) of my smile, assured that the average customer could refuse only at the cost of half an hour's rending guilt and a broken heart. In a month 'Mr. Marshal' was telling me I 'was one of his best boys'. As a matter of fact I had checked up and knew better. I was his *best* boy, (best only in a certain sense related to the Capitalist System, you will understand). I had the longest weekly paper route in town. My treacherous selling methods were only one part of the story. The main secret was that the other boys worked only in their own neighbourhoods, or neighbourhoods where they were known. I worked all neighbourhoods. To explain this I again have to go back a little.

As a little lad, dating from about five on, I was quite a fighter. Mind you I didn't say I was a good fighter: in fact I was one of the worst fighters I have ever known. I mean, I was an *enthusiastic* fighter. Size, strength, reputation, didn't bother me in the least. The moment I heard the slightest imputation against my honour (nuances so fine that the average *Irish* chap couldn't detect them) I was in there with my fists flying like a dog doing the paddle. I'm not kidding you. That's exactly how I fought in the first place, like a swimmer doing the paddle. (I couldn't swim.) Naturally, especially as I was a sickly child, I took a hell of a beating almost daily. But I wouldn't quit. Had a strong bone structure, flesh like the original superman (I never got a bruise in my life, unless a bone was actually broken — for instance, I have never had a black eye). Didn't need to quit. There was one exception to this. My nose was weak. One whack to the nose and I would bleed like a pig. I wasn't entirely beyond reason. One smack on the nose and I would immediately surrender. On the other hand I developed sophisticated methods of protecting my nose. Nevertheless I developed no methods of protecting other parts of my body (they didn't need them): and took a terrible series of lickings. I couldn't even beat a boy two years younger than me, if he was stocky. This was because my Dad had told me never to use an uppercut. If you used an uppercut you were liable to break somebody's neck. As if my feeble blows could break anybody's neck. Anybody should know you can't hit a fighter shorter than you except with an uppercut. This was one of the things I didn't know. I told you I was smart, true, but only smart in certain ways. Not in fighting.

Later in a book (or in THE TORONTO STAR WEEKLY, my first move on any sales trip was to read the thing from cover to cover) I read an article on scientific boxing. The chief lesson of that book or article was *use your left*. I used my left all right. I used my left with such one-sided concentration that I forgot entirely about my right. Naturally all the opponent had to do was to circle around to his left (my right) and pound the piss out of me. Nevertheless I wouldn't give up. And by this time my ability to protect my nose had become phenomenal. I still wouldn't give up. The final result of almost any fight would be for my opponent to drop his hands, say "you sure can take it!" and like as not walk away — as tired as he cared to be. The final result after the final result was equally inevitable. Boys came from all over town to see if they could make Mickey Acorn quit. After all what could they lose? It was a tempting challenge and furthermore absolutely safe.

It's an ill wind which won't blow you some good if you stand in it long enough and catch at things as they go past. This time I'm talking of was the very pit of the Depression. One of my childhood friends had actually died from a combination of starvation and exposure. That was in the past (though recent) now. P.E.I. not only had a system of relief going (much better, judging by final physical results, than the other provinces) but was shipping carloads of provisions to the Prairies. If I may boast of my native province, this, to the Islanders, was not philanthropy but plain and simple logic. If you can't sell your produce you might as well give it away. Murderers could reform and regain their reputation, but wastrels never. However though the Depression distress on P.E.I. was only comparative — for the children of the poor — there was a decided lack of pocket money. There were child beggars everywhere you went — and it was just like being in the depths of Darkest Hindustan. If you were unwise enough to yield to one of them's 'give me a cent' a whole swarm of them would immediately be after you, demanding their portion. They could be persistent and abusive, fights could start.

Other impoverished youth went for a bolder approach. They needed pocket money. Who had money in their pockets? Newsboys. Newsboys had money in their pockets. Newsboys were fair game. That's why the other newsboys generally worked in neighborhoods where they were known and had friends. I however had a friend on every block . . . because I had fought them all! One or two good fights and two boys are generally friends for life. That's a well-known law of nature. If I happened to get caught with no protectors in sight, I had another trick. I carried a change-purse. I *did not* carry my money in the change purse. I carried it in my pockets. But when faced with the threat of robbery I would with an air of the most solemn certitude pull out the change purse, open it and show the bandit that it was empty. By the time the young fellow had this figured out, there would be a crowd of interested spectators around and his chance was gone. If all this failed I made a surprising discovery about myself . . . Where money was concerned I could fight like a wildcat. It didn't matter then if my nose bled or not. The tangle would be so thick the other lad would start imagining it was his own blood. One memorable case I recall frequently, and never recall without chuckling. A boy hit me on the nose. He dropped his fists and said, "Oh boy! Right on the nose!" Naturally the next punch was mine, and in fact the last. His mouth was bleeding before my nose was, and much worse.

Of course there were exceptions. There was one poor young psychopath who was the smartest boy in his class — also the poorest. He used to spend half his time in reform school and the other half taking revenge on the world. With him I used yet another and subtler psychology. There would be a short scuffle. No damage done. Then I would solemnly aver that he had won, but accuse him of winning by a foul blow. He considered no compliment greater than being called a dirty fighter. As for money, he wasn't interested in such small amounts as I carried. He was of the aristocracy — a juvenile delinquent . . .

There was one other exception. A whole area — Boughton. To this day I never use the name of the Boughton district of Charlottetown as a noun. I use it as an adjective; and the noun is 'vermin'. Boughton was the abode of such small representation of the middle class as we had in Charlottetown in those days. In the middle class one has no friends, only acquaintances and rivals. This applies equally as much to the children as the parents. Middle class children are now 'dropping out' in large numbers. They weren't in those days. For a strange boy, especially a strange poor boy, to appear in Boughton was literally risking death. Those young rats had no idea of fair play. They'd come at you in bunches. They would pummel you til you went down. When you went down they would jump on you. How come none of them ever stove in a rib, is something for which I must thank my guardian angel, or else my strong bone structure. However, as in the previous case, they were not interested in my money. They got plenty from their parents. Besides, stealing was wrong. They wouldn't begin to question the ethics of their fathers until their twenties or thirties. Then they would go in for embezzlement. So, after they'd had their fun I would lie there recovering for a while, get up, plug my bleeding nose with some cotton wool I always carried; and went on delivering my Boughton papers. I don't know whether the word for this is 'stupid' or 'stubborn'. Unlike Rocky Graziano, I can't say that somebody up there likes me; but sometimes, in my mystical moments I think somebody up there was preparing me for a hard life. I don't think it was God himself. I think it was just some minor angel in the bureaucracy who just got away too enthusiastic.

Now comes the part of my tale of co-adventure where I must go back to the first. That matter of half-a-cent. The reduction of the 'carriers' (newsboys') share of the retail dime from the 3 3/4 cents I mentioned recently to the 3¼ cents I mentioned in the first place. I often wonder what was the reason. Was it that the newsboy's 3 3/4 cents was actually more than the STAR's competitors were giving? That the STAR WEEKLY had been putting on a circulation drive, aiming its guns primarily at the newsboys; and now that the circulation had reached its optimum: it was time for the STAR to start drawing on its main source of income — *worker's blood?* Or was it entirely a concern of H.M. Marshal & Company? Who had noted that in Charlottetown (and no doubt other places) certain newsboys were making sales miraculously greater than others . . . and in one of those magnificent feats of deduction typical of the Canadian Capitalist class — instant deduction without a suggestion of investigation — had concluded that the majority of 'carriers' were lazy? Had me and other newsboys with special advantages like mine, in our childish innocence *forced up the quota?* Sometime in my old age, when more important things are less pressing, I must investigate that particular intance of the devilish exploitation established and handed down from on high as OUR WAY OF LIFE! I even have a suspicion the decision originated right there in Charlottetown; that the underpaid clerk I insisted on calling 'Mr. Marshal' had thought perhaps to remedy his underpayment by arranging more underpayment for the children in his charge? Thus gaining the approval of those lofty and beneficent powers whom we all knew existed aloft? I'll probably never know. It'll probably never be worth knowing.

But there was something about the way he sat behind his microscopic desk, like a skinny pharoah lacking a throne; how his lips moved as if actually carved out of stone and yet by some marvel still capable of moving . . . something about his starched shirt and neat brown tie that bugged me anyway. *"Cast your bread upon the waters . . ."* That's what the Bible said and I had read it. "I quit!" I said.

"Now wait a minute," said 'Mr. Marshal', "You're being foolish. Besides, don't you know your paper route is a valuable property . . . If you're tired of it you can sell it to another boy." Sure it was a valuable property. Especially at 6 3/4 cents out of a dime to the wholesaler. I didn't say that. Don't even know if I thought it. But as I left I allowed myself one quick look over my shoulder and for the first time in my life smiled at him. I had heard of strikes of course. But strikes were something that happened in Cape Breton, not Prince Edward Island — besides how could you organize a strike of newsboys? I had also heard of sabotage.

My father and I had many bitter quarrels. I'm not referring to mere "you're one — you're another and worse besides" verbal encounters or even spankings, tho both occurred. I'm referring to actual all-out combat. Psychological studies have shown that such a bring-up never really harms the final result — the man; as long as the coercion is consistent. My Dad was inconsistent. "Don't dare raise your hand to me!" The key word was *dare*. Tho the old man never seemed to realize that. Up would come my hand and I'd get the proverbial old fertilizer beat out of me. Up til I was sixteen or so my father always won. But sometimes I made a good showing. Was my father disappointed? You can bet your life he wasn't. He'd go around boasting for days. In my presence yet! Once in his presence I had a hot argument with my school principal. Did I get a bawling out for disrespect to my elders? (Besides the fact the principal was right.) No sir, I got congratulations for sticking up for what I thought was right. On the other hand I *did* get many bawlings out for disrespect to my elders. Small wonder that today my 'nerves' are bad (sometimes I live for weeks on tranquilizers and Southern Comfort) but my 'nerve' is fantastic. Sometimes I look with amazement at one or another of the things I've done — for no other reason than because I thought it was right — and am amazed again that no shiver runs down my spine . . . I recall each and every moment as one of the happiest of my life: leaving out certain sexual moments that is.

So my father didn't react with fury at me quitting a job and reducing the family's finances. He even further reduced them by again paying me an allowance. His tolerance may have come a bit from the fact that he's gone thru that romanticized infantile hell of being a newsboy in his time — in fact been the main support of his family, which I wasn't. But that wasn't what was important. I had quit on a matter of principle. That was what was important. So our discussion of this was amazingly mild. A few words here. A few words there. Pauses that went on for hours, days, weeks. At one point he said "Mr. (the fellow I called Mr. Marshal — damned if I'd call him anything else) keeps asking about you. He says you were one of his best boys!" At that I came as near exploding as I ever did in the argument. "Sure I'm his best boy — but why should I go tramping around with a load in the sun and the rain while he sits in a nice office with a white shirt and — "

I stopped in mid-sentence, interrupted not by my Dad but my own sudden thoughts. It was not a nice office. It was a lousy office. A shack. Hot in summer, cold in winter. I had seen good offices and knew the difference. As for Mr. What's-His-Name, he wasn't just sitting there in a white shirt and tie . . . he was starving there in a white shirt and tie. MY BOSS — to whose instructions I paid not the slightest attention; sat there with a tiny portion of HIS BOSS's brains clamped down over his head like a baseball cap on the waterboy . . . and nothing else to think with! All this didn't go thru my head all at once. After all I was only twelve years old. But the germs of all those things were all there. At the risk of the reader developing a sudden itch in the asshole and going no farther — I must say that I was beginning to make a class analysis.

My father said nothing. I said nothing. I went back to work. What was the use of 'striking' all by yourself? My boss ceased to be called Mr. Marshall. I went thru all sorts of circumlocutions to keep from calling him "Hey You!"

All this I got away with. I was top hand and I knew it. THE STAR WEEKLY people might have figured the town was saturated with their lousy treacherous rag, and robbed the newsboys for that reason; but within a few weeks I proved them wrong. I was walking a longer route at the end than I had before.

The end came not at the hands of an enemy, but of a couple of friends. I told you at the start I was a sickly boy. The reason was that I had a truly remarkable and interesting pair of tonsils: remarkable, interesting and . . . dangerous. The local doctors had been waiting for years for a certain new kind of a specialist to finish his training . . . a specialist who could remove those tonsils without killing me.

Before going into hospital I made what I thought were all the arrangements necessary. My three concerns — as to anybody who would take over my route whilst I was laid up, were (1) could he fight (2) did he have brains (3) did he have nerve? I picked what I thought was a perfect choice. A fellow a year older than me, stronger than me, quicker with his hands and feet than me, and almost as quick with his tongue. With confidence far more serene than that of the doctors I went into the hospital. Came out in triumph about a week later. In two weeks more I felt myself recuperated and went back to reclaim my route. My favoured choice was reduced to eight customers — not even the same eight. In order to get the right answers you must ask the right questions — all of them. In my list of mental questions before taking on this helper I had forgotten one . . . (4) what did he like — girls or boys? Now the fact the fellow liked boys did not make the slightest difference to me. "Chacun à son gout" has always been my motto. Besides I hardly knew what sex was, let alone homosexuality. But the Irish lads of the town who had always protected me not only knew, but had definite opinions on the subject — opinions upon which they were prepared to act. Whereas I had had a protector in just about every block, he had a raging foe at about every crack in the pavement. My substitute could fight — there was no doubt about that — but not ten bouts a day. Why I myself had never been able to manage more than two or three.

(I didn't figure this out at the time. I was still far too green. For years I went around hating him for a slacker and a person of no honour. When realization came to me I wanted to go to him and apologize. But how could you put an apology of that nature into words?) Half-heartedly I started trying to build a route again; but it was no use. The STAR had built up its circulation by posing as a friend of labour. Its employees had taken that so seriously that they'd gone on strike themselves. The strike broken . . . THE STAR decided on a safer policy . . . . Not to be a friend of labour in Canada, but a friend of labour in Russia — where the working class was presumably in power. Nationally this brought the WEEKLY into a slow decline. In Charlottetown the decline — or at least the chance of finding new customers — was as sudden as falling of a cliff on a moonless night. The locals had caught on immediately. As Al Purdy says:

"Russian Steel production figures at Roblin Lake (or Charlottetown) . . . *were exactly nil".*

In his book THE WHITE NIGGERS OF AMERICA, Pierre Vallières speaks with a sort of honorary sadness about the Communists of the Angus Shops in his days. I wish I could tell you about those Angus Shops Communist sympathizers and what they did to the Party. But that's another story; and besides the Angus Shop Story did result in one shining victory for Communism or Socialism or whatever you want to call it — the education of Pierre Vallières. Similarly Old Joe Whiskers gained one slight advantage from the catastrophe the STAR WEEKLY suffered in Charlottetown. I read those articles — Russian steel production and all that. I read them and pondered them. Knowing the source I was not (and never have been) a firm believer. My conclusion was those stories might be right and might be wrong — but the idea was certainly possible. Could human beings co-operate and create a better society? Well human beings had certainly co-operated and let me run my paper route. All my jungle cunning would have

gained me nothing, had I not had friends and protectors —
and (here's the nub): My protectors had been one and all
working class. So I thought, but vaguely and abstractly . . .
since the only steel I possessed was in the nails of my shoes
and the knife in my pocket: which steel was not at all Russian, but Canadian and perfectly good.

It was not the STAR WEEKLY which made a Commie
out of me. It was TRUE DETECTIVE. Not its contents.
Detective stories of any kind have always bored me. Just the
picture on the front page and the headline
EXPOSED! COMMUNIST PLOT TO BLOW UP
THE CAPITOL!
Underneath was portrayed a secret agent, (whether Russian
or American wasn't specified, but I presumed he was a
Russian) entering a room full of poison gas, with a gas mask
on and firing a revolver. I started to form a boy's fantasy on
that, putting myself firstly in the place of the Americans.
But suddenly my eyes went back to that word 'CAPITOL'

This thing is of wondrous telling
I hit the truth by a mistake in spelling

There was this thing called 'Capitolism.' It had a head-
quarters called the 'Capitol.' The Communists were out to
blow up the 'Capitol.' Thus putting an end to 'Capitolism.'
That beat Russian steel statistics all to hell! In the wink of
an eye I was fantasizing from the opposite side, tho from the
Communist side, not the Russian. No sir. I was the heroic
Canadian Communist. One of the breed who stormed Vimy
Ridge. Who took Teruel and then had it taken back as soon
as their backs were turned.

I cannot say I never looked back. From then on I looked
front and sideways, up and down, back and outside, inside
too. Never front and centre. Front and centre is a bourgeois
concept. But from that day forward I knew who I was.

Sonnet in Hot Pursuit of Chaucer

It's late October and the sap's retreating
From blanching twigs, limbs and trunks
Down past the frostline to set roots drunk
With power necessary for growth underneath
Cold's gelid breathlessness and pounding breath
Unseething quiet ice and whispering snow.
Shifting below, breaking new ground to sheath
New roots; the trees, I theorize, move slow to Spring
As we humans grow, or lose our youth.
The birds and bosses are flying south;
Some to play and some to hatch a second brood . . .
Some to plot the devil knows what cheating.

Whatever's good in us will be tested
While our hearts take the place of the sun:
For ours is not the kingdom. Ours is the power
In these cursed and cursing months, weeks and hours,
To direct the winter storms in our heads.
So one day, when they come back, tanned with will and wit
To seize April . . . We'll have taken it.

Lapse

Driving to hot Montreal, from the mountains
In a thickening, slowing traffic stream —
As routine convoys sail toward submarines;
The glazing glare gets me to drowse; half-dream.

I'm in a bauble-flaunting, proud parade
Jauntily feathered, bright shell-hung, near naked
Singing as we step strong, slightly upgrade.
We are in our own world. Our songs make it
Take shape, proportion to reverberate long.
We jump, we stomp, we whirl, we are so strong.

A horn blares frightened rage. It's a near miss
Snapping off my thought, to steer grinning awry
To second thoughts of boredom, in such simplicity . . .
But what the hell is life for? Is it this?

After Kim Chi Ha: Jailed in South Korea

(from: 'PARTING')

I couldn't sleep a night not stunned drunk
Or make it safe through a day with no fight
Til a needle bit me, and my soul shrunk
Whispering my shadow a faint goodnight
As the poor worn creature disappeared.
Then I woke and saw a very strange land
Where wind fretted over fallen shacks and
Cut to bloody strips, my youth was interred.

Yellow sunrays tore up the yellow ground —
Dug me out to hug tomorrow's struggle.
Rise with this sun my friends! Again juggle
Our lives and deaths as fists of fate to pound
Those rotbottomed tyrants til they're downed.

What I Know of God is This

What I know of God is this:
That He has hands, for He touches me.
I can testify to nothing else;
Living among many unseen beings
Like the whippoorwill I'm constantly hearing
But was pointed out to me just once.

Last of our hopes whan all hope's past
God, never let me call on Thee
Distracting myself from a last chance
Which goes just as quick as it comes;
And I have doubts of Your omnipotence.
All I ask is . . . Keep on existing
Keeping Your hands. Continue to touch me.

Poem of One of the Poems for Which Kenneth Leslie was Damned

To the Red Miners of the Princess Shaft
Moses Coady came. Tim Buck had turned his back
On them. Big Jim MacLauchlin laughed,
Cursed, wept, roared until a final hack-
Ing cough burst to time the bursting of his heart.
Now could the Communists and radical priest
Meet challenge to challenge. What brave parts
Were taken and spoken? We should know that at least.

The minutes of course are terse and obscure
In places we precisely want to know.
Dumb coward history! Who now can cure
The scar put on memory forty-odd years ago?
Kenneth Leslie, poet, wrote it long and strong-lunged.
For this duty, critics ripped out his tongue.

Lord Who Let That Oldtime Cosmic Egg

Lord who let that oldtime cosmic egg go
Bust and scatter poor me all across heaven;
Balanced the great globe itself on top of my spine:
To be or not to be ain't no question;
But if I bowed my head, what would happen?
How many are in this situation?
What if we bowed our heads all at once?
What if we looked up and saw the sky gone
Because those overweighted heads had all dropped off?
I can hear those practical fellows scoff
"Nothing ever existed — You poor dunce . . . "

Incident With Stompin Tom

Before a firing squad of gunbarrel eyes, Tom
Sang — let's face it — not his greatest song
. . . one which those murdering scabs had forbidden
(what's life not dared living to the rules of freedom?)
But I waffle, re and disargue;
How many letters of how many names will stick strong
Together in memory's bowl of alphabet soup?
Don't stance and circumstance, courage count too?

If birth had given me no eyes at all
Or ears, voice or sense. If I wasn't
Here, there or anything much: a black hole
In the present flex of time would draw
Another into the space of my absent presence
To shout in lawful lawlessness the true law.

My Big Heart

(after Hikmet)
Doctor listened with his stethoscope
To my inner machinery, and said
"You've got a big heart; thumping out time
All around your chest."
                          I said, "Yes I know
Since every undeservedly aimed blow
Ever driven at anyone has hit it."

"It's swelling all the time with hope
For this one, that one, others popping out
From wombs firing like machine-guns;
Each new person jumped and mugged for profit,
Learning language by hearing himself cursed
For being here and ever having done
Anything except for a bully's gain:
Starting with the crime of birth."

"Doctor: It's for a bomb I need this big heart
To smash those liars into a great squashed stain
When the pressure jumps too much, and it blows apart."

If You Wont Live

If you won't live your own dreams I claim
All which belongs to this damned land I love;
Though all the souls you've expelled
From your blood's own warmth, hustle and shove
Into mine . . . Til each swimming cell has a name
Which should have been yours, and a mouth
To spit those bolts of truth you won't impel.

If Québec leaves Confederation and slides into the maw of the United States, what is lost? The whole country is slipping into the maw of the United States; and it's through Confederation this vile devourment is being accomplished.

If Québec leaves Confederation, establishes her independence; while the rest of the country slides into the maw of the United States; then one country is saved from American Imperialism. Since Canada is going fast anyway, there's net gain.

If Québec leaves Confederation, establishes her independence; and by her example inspires Canadians to strive for and win independence; then there is a double gain.

If partly in consequence of Québec leaving Confederation
both Canada and Québec slide into the maw of the United
States; nothing is really lost because that's the situation
anyway. It's only a question of formality and degree.

> Rise Canadians! To flip on your stomachs
> Like snakes or multiple cords of a whip.
> Squirm to the charmpipes of the U.S.A.
> Letting your blood squirt south, sip-a-drip . . .
> Content to live as worms in her excrement;
> Loosing your resentment on Québec
> Pardon me if my decoded tongue
> Won't obfuscate the cowardice you vent.

Invocation

You loved one, hurt one, loving one still strong . . .
If you were only an impossible vision
Why would you lurk — a quiet worm in my tongue
Wait and live to raise this invocation?
What did you look through, in Spook Canyon
Besides that smiling mask, carved from a tree —
Tools learning as they cut a growing wisdom
To top and ornament your poor wronged body?
You have entered me, dead but not done.

I've loved, and love the Earth. If you are Death
Stay around to summon more performance.
Is that smile kinder yet? Plumbing consent?
Wait for the laughter! It'll blow breath
Tumbling all your atoms to collect 'em
Til lungs pump, your heart flutters, eyes go wide
And I'll be wise, at last, to find a bride.
My vehicle accelerates, bright one. Come.

Credits

Sonnet Translated from the Gaelic
Canada East

A Winning Young Lad of Can-Po
After Kim Chi Ha: Jailed in South Korea
Love in the Nineteen Fifties
The Montreal Fan
No Music from the Bar
Poem Beginning with a Quote from Heracleitus
Sonnet Written Coldly Lest I Cry
The Wake-Up Raven
(*Canadian Forum*)

If You Won't Live
Canadian Voice

The Man from Headless Valley
Copperfield

Poem of One of the Poems for Which Kenneth Leslie Was
    Damned
To a Goddam Boss
CV II

The Waterhole
Gut

Rose in Absence
The Island Means Minago

Incident with Stompin Tom
Our True/False National Anthem
To Joe's Last Grunt
It needs to be said

Celebrate the Battle of the Little Big Horn
Prairie Star
The Fourth Estate

By Still More Stubborn Stars
First Wife Sonnet
Shoot Yourself or Shit Yourself
The Minor Poet with the Major Voice
Scarborough Echo

My Life as a Co-adventurer
This Magazine